Seven Seasons

Seven Seasons

Collected poems

by Detelina Stoykova-Asenov

MindMend Publishing

Published in 2019 by the
MindMend Publishing Co., New York, NY

Copyright © 2019 by Detelina Stoykova-Asenov

All rights reserved.

For permissions to reproduce more than 100 words of this publication, email to ORIPressEditor@gmail.com or write to MindMend Publishing Editor @ 7515 187th St, Fresh Meadows, NY 11366.

Printed in the United States of America on acid free paper.

Library of Congress Control Number: 2019943405

Cataloging Data:

Stoykova-Asenov, Detelina. Seven Seasons: Collection of Poems/ Detelina Stoykova-Asenov

1. Language arts and disciplines/ Writing/ Poetry. 2. Psychobiography. 3. Conscious and unconscious communications. 4. Creativity (literary, artistic, etc.) – Psychological concepts.

ISBN-13: 978-1-942431-14-5 (soft cover)

Cover drawing by Penko Platikanov
Drawings by Penko Platikanov and Valentina Asenov
Editing by Summar West
Head shot photo on back cover by Alex Antonov
Book design, copy editing, and book cover - by MindMendMedia, Inc. @ MindMendMedia.com

To my loved ones

"Skip the imperfections if you want to find the truth…"
Daniel – my love, my strength

TABLE OF CONTENTS

PREFACE (xiii)

I. REFLECTIONS

CONTEMPLATION (3)
REFLECTION (6)
LIVING AT THE SHORE (7)
NIGHT CREATURES (8)
COMPASS (9)
MEMORY OF CHRISTMAS (10)
UNDONE (10)
HEAVENLY SILKWORM (11)

II. MINIATURES AND HAIKU FROM THE SHORE

CIRCLE (15)
THE OCEAN'S LIKE A LAKE TODAY (16)
SPRING CLEAN (16)
ONCE IN A WHILE (17)
ROSE (17)
I WISH THE MORNING LASTED LONGER (17)
MEETING (18)
WHEREVER WE GO THERE IT IS (18)
THE SUN PATH (19)
MORNING (19)
AT THE JETTY (19)
LAUGHING BUDDHA (20)
DARK PERFUME (20)
NOT THERE (20)
FREEDOM IS (21)
AT THE PERIMETER (21)
SURRENDER I (22)
SURRENDER II (22)
INDIAN SUMMER (23)
THRONE (23)

BLOSSOMS (23)
SPRING OCEAN (24)
WARM ROCKS (24)
TEMPLE (24)
ANCIENT MEMORY (25)
LIMPING SEAGULL (25)
SHARE THE ROCKS (25)
LIGHTHEARTED (25)
THE SCENT OF THE BEACH (26)
LAZY AFTERNOON (26)
JEWELED SUNRISE (26)
WHEN AT THE OCEAN (27)
BLUE IRISES (27)

III. TO MY LOVED

PASSION (31)
DEAR BEAR (32)
A STAR IS BORN (33)
A DAY OF LOVE (34)
THE RAIN IS FALLING (35)
KALEIDOSCOPE (36)
CHEST COLD (38)
I AM YOUR TOWN (38)
MONDAY SONG (39)
DUET (40)
THE POEMS I'VE GIVEN AWAY (41)
TEN BALLOONS (42)
TO MY MOM (43)
HEART LEFT BEHIND (45)
TELL THEM (46)

IV. NEW ROMANTICS

POETRY CORNER (49)
LOVE IS... (50)
IS IT AN ANCIENT INCANTATION? (50)
TANGO IS (51)

TO THE TANGO LESSON (52)
MORNING RHYTHM (53)
I SEE SADNESS IN HIS EYES (55)
CORAZON (56)
AFTER THE TAKEN (57)
PLEA (58)
LOVE IS ONLY FOR THE BRAVE (59)
PORTRAIT (60)
NO HIDING IN THAT ONE (61)
IN THE EMBRACE (62)
NIGHT SONG (63)
SAY WHAT YOU WILL (64)
POT OF MILK (65)

V. ODES

ODE ABOUT AN OLD CROW (69)
LITTLE BEIGE PANT (71)
THE DAY IS LONG (74)

VI. DREAMS

DREAM I (83)
DREAM II (84)
A DREAM IN FILM NOIR (85)

VII. TRANSLATED POEMS

I LOVED YOU, BY ALEXANDER PUSHKIN (89)
PRAYER, BY MIKHAIL LERMONTOV (90)
SONG OF MY SONG, BY PEYO YAVOROV (91)
TWO BEAUTIFUL EYES, BY PEYO YAVOROV (94)
TWO SOULS, BY PEYO YAVOROV (95)
TO LORA, BY PEYO YAVOROV (96)
GAZE TOWARD THE STARS, BY ILIYA STOYKOV (97)

APPENDIX

LIST OF DRAWINGS (101)
NOTES ON POEMS AND TRANSLATIONS (101)
ABOUT THE AUTHOR (103)

PREFACE

All art is at once surface and symbol.
Those who go beneath the surface do so at their peril....
Those who read the symbol do so at their peril
— Oscar Wilde

We live simultaneously in different layers of reality — the material, which some consider to be the "real" reality, and the subtler ones — intellectual, emotional and spiritual. Poetry takes its inspiration from the very concrete and visible world, uplifts it to the intangible, and then brings it back to the material form, dressed in words. Poetry takes us beyond words, and what it embodies becomes "real", connecting and transcending the concrete and the intangible.

Poetry reveals and conceals at the same time. Poetry finds beautiful words for beautiful things; and poetry finds beautiful words for ugly things. It is the spectator who will translate into their own language the material and intangible imagery that transpires through the poems.

These poems were written during a span of more than twenty years. This selection is significant, as for the first time, I have decided to tie together loose ends and put my poems into a coherent whole. Though they come from different times in my life and from different places on the globe, a consistent thread runs throughout — they incorporate my experience in the world, Old and New, where living authentically often required leaving oneself behind, and discovering, and creating a new self. Awaiting the revelation of who I become is a part of that journey. To be vulnerable and daring, ethical and immoral, virtuous and unapologetic is the lifeblood of art, and the artist has to find the courage to register everything and to express unarmed confessions — in jubilant songs of romance or in the white verse of quietness.

The name *Seven Seasons* came from the Atlantic shores, which have been my home for the last twenty years. The subtlety of the changing seasons here, more distinctly noticeable than any other place in the world — with its multitude of soft shades —

gives the impression that in between the four seasons there resides something more, when the change from one season to the other occurs. This transition in muted undertones, as well as the change from day to night or night to day is the inspiration for many of the haiku and miniature poems, alluding to the seasons of the heart and the seasons of life. In the atmosphere of this hour of the dusk, in the neither-here-nor-there, eternity exists in the present. The haunting light of these moments breaks through into the other, intangible layers of reality which only poetry can capture. The connectedness between body, mind and emotions, between human beings and between human beings and nature, pulsates in this collection in an apotheosis of Love that sustains all life.

Detelina Stoykova-Asenov
Ocean City, NJ
February, 2019

I. REFLECTIONS

Light where you are
Dark where you're not…

CONTEMPLATION

I took some time off
of my life,
I needed to go
I needed to do some
soul searching.
The sky was arching
for days with the rain
turning the shore into marshes.
I needed to see
what has troubled me,
what has gone down the trails of
                              my heart.
My body remained
in the concrete plain
in the life where I knew that you were;
But I couldn't stay there
I needed to veer.
The ravenous minutes
kept piling up
seconds beating like bells...
finding my way back
through the tracks of the past
was no easy task.
I visited places
long forgotten
faces flashing
along the way
some friendly
some sinister
fields filled with dark visitors
lingering figures...
I bet you didn't know
you thought I was a virgin
in all that dark stuff,
that it didn't bother me,

you thought I was
pure and fragile...
Yet tough
from traveling
I wonder where it all began
was it when I knifed the fear
at the edge of the garden
in that childhood haze
with the night –
only witness to my bravery?
It remained there
in a distant frontier...
and back in the cities
where free and pretty
I hitchhiked
with crowds of friends
on roads and highways
finding our ways to the sea
moonlit nights and the strings of guitars
and the screams of despair
flames of bright charcoal
flaring up in the air
above the dunes where we slept
like mad children...
Then the love...
the departure the ocean the sky and the shore
that invited us all
dream-like and surreal...
What began as a dream was now real.
Was it real?
I was not afraid
I wasn't intending to stay...
But I'm here...
I'll be back with first light
when the rain has subsided
and the clouds have moved away
leaving only the morning dew

my face will emerge
bright and new
for a new day
where I hope
I can still find
you...

REFLECTION

"Where love ends poetry begins" –
I'm tired of this story
Of death
And mourning
Of visiting
The chambers of despair
Anesthetized suffering
A temple for masochists
To feel sorry

"Where love sparks poetry begins." –
Writing our stories
With our fleeting meetings
salvaging ourselves
From disappearing
Into timelessness…

A stranger said:
"I heard you say I love you to
                              someone else
and I felt loved..."

LIVING AT THE SHORE

Living at the shore
it's a chance
unlike living inland
every day washes anew
with the tides and the ebbs,
the morning dew
and the night which pulls through
the veil of the setting sun
by the bay.

The moon is always immense
and one never knows what the winds
                          might blow,
every morning we walk outside
to find out what the tide might bring,
and every night we open our windows
to hear what the breeze might sing.

In the morning
maidens send their beloved
to sea with the nets,
in the evening they will return
with a catch or regrets.

It's different here at the perimeter
where sometimes there are stars
and sometimes there are none...

NIGHT CREATURES

The roofs are breathing
Dark creatures
With glistening scales
Refracting
The moon dust and star dust
Sprinkling down
On them
They squeak
Poised
Ready to take off
To lift upwards
In their nightly flights
To places unknown...
Come morning
With the first lights
Of the dawn
They'd settle again
In repose
Awaiting
For the dusk

COMPASS

I'm going East
I'm going South
I'm going North
I'm going West...

You might recall all of the rest...

They say back in time
We had within us
An internal compass
Long ago
We knew
Where North was
And how to go...

A tiny black bird
Speckled in white
Stood on a wire
Spelled out its song
And took up in flight...
She knew where North was...

I smiled at the Universe
The Universe smiled back at me

MEMORY OF CHRISTMAS
(after Emily Dickinson)

When frosty hills are tinted rose
Receding into the night
An orange pill on wooden stove
Is crackling inside.

Behind the windows wet with steam
From popping white popcorn
Just like the snow piled up
In front of the house door.

The air thick with butter sweet
orange and smoke and resin tree
was Christmas then for me...

UNDONE

I learned a thing today –
have you ever undone a knot?
No matter how entangled
a knot might seem
it got to be like this
in certain way the strings went
therefore, it can be
undone
by gently
reversing it
only one has to carefully
follow the direction of the strings
and after a while when it all looks
really knotty
with a single move –
the whole thing unravels...

HEAVENLY SILKWORM

A faint star
at the horizon
mere speck
enveloped in darkness
a heavenly
silkworm
inching its way
to the moon
but the moon –
strolling
magnificent
through
dusky clouds
ever higher
the faint star
aiming upwards
captured in
her nebular light
it shone ever brighter
acquiring a veil
of white gauze
until it glared
like a sun
in the vicinity
of the cool disk

Glorious
Fainting

II. MINIATURES AND HAIKU FROM THE SHORES

Haiku expresses the stillness of the center.
There is no conflict in Haiku.

Circle

I breathe the earth
the shore the dunes
I host the birds
within myself
the green waves
washing on the rocks
all lay within me
and then they have me
the sand my steps
will keep forever
entangled atoms
wash ashore
the rock my weight will carry
the waves my particles
will spread throughout the oceans
they will evaporate
with sea foam
and rain down once more,

I breathe the earth
I host the birds
the rocks
the green waves
within myself...

The Ocean's Like a Lake Today

The ocean's like a lake today
I met a woman
who said she was ok
I did sun prayer on the rocks
and found forget-me-nots.

Water's trickling under my feet
like a deep well is beneath.
A flock of birds just flew by –
Black arrow in the silky sky...
Life is beautiful!..

Spring Clean

Appreciating the time
I have
for spring cleaning
today
the gallery of memories
the pictures
on the walls
the plant trimming
and how
I want to rearrange
them all
in a new way...

Once in a While

once in a while
you look through the window
and see
the clouds moving...

Rose

morning sun
behind the rocky hill –
blazing rose
beneath
the seagull's wings

I Wish the Morning Lasted Longer

I wish the morning
lasted longer
the air crisp
the quiet
the misty aroma
wet earth and early ocean
steaming gently
from the night's dew

Meeting

I came to the Ocean today
and the Ocean
came to me

*Wherever We Go
There It Is*

when in the morning you go to the sea
you see the sun path,
start walking along
and the sun path moves along
you cannot leave it behind
everyone who walks there
close by or away
is also by the sun path's way
it is deceptive to think
that everyone
who's not by our side
is not by
the sun path.
We are afraid to move
from fear not to lose the path or each other
but it is clear
it is there for us all along
as well as for another
then we realize that everyone else
not by our side
is also on the sun path
and wherever we go there it is –
next time you're there
try this…

The Sun Path

I went to the sun path –
it was there for me.

       ***

walking along the sun path
to the East –
it's always by your side

Morning

running spirited towards
the boardwalk
saying good morning to the
early workers and the fisherman

At the Jetty

the jetty is my friend
who offers me a throne to sit
and share the
horizon with
the sea gulls...

Laughing Buddha

my Dad's image appeared
in the morning haze
like a soft laughing Buddha
soft laughing Buddha

Dark Perfume

the night breathes a dark perfume
revealing its secrets to the
enlightened ones

Not there

the fog transforms the shore colors
to a subtle bareness
almost not there…

Freedom is

the tiny grass blade
bending with the wind
twirling back and forth
now aiming straight up
gently trembling like a string
played by the breeze
laying close to the earth
and flying up again
following every which way
the wind takes it
without resistance.

what freedom...

At the Perimeter

'cause we rather live on the tips
of the platform
and love and admire the view

Surrender I

between the sunset
and the moonrise
twisting waves
slowly become smaller and calmer
until the ocean succumbs
to the night
prostrating
a glossy surface
for the moon
to shine

Surrender II

through the dusky veil
of the sunset
the moon was shyly
presenting herself
to the ocean surface
dusting its way
with silvery glitter

Indian Summer

again, the beach is mine
the summer crowds gone
leaving the waves behind
talking gently to the shore...

Throne

I sat in the lap
of a tree
roots swirling around me
from Earth to the air
reaching up
enveloping rocks
dipping down dry ends
in the creek...

Blossoms

ablaze are the tops
of the white blossoms
nip in the air

***

glowing white
blossoming trees
in the crisp morning air

Spring Ocean

spring Ocean
pearled
swelling
washing on the glistening
rocks

Warm Rocks

though the air is brisk
the rocks are
warm
with the first sun

Temple

the dawn is a temple
of red glow
a seagull posed
on the pillar –
the only witness of the sacrament
waiting for the Sun...

Ancient memory

Somewhere
on the ancient streets
I'll meet the woman
of my dreams
who climbed the steps
toward the sky or sea
and found a treasure
and met the woman
of her dreams...

Limping Seagull

a limping seagull
by the shore
but still –
it took off in flight

Share the Rocks

sharing the rocks
with the birds
while the storm's
out in the ocean

Lighthearted

sometimes
you look through the window
and see the clouds moving

The Scent of the Beach

I wrapped the last day on the beach
in my towel.
I will open it in winter –
Sun screen
Salt
Wet bathing suit
and this faint smell
of blown up
Floaties...

Lazy Afternoon

lazy afternoon
easy Latino music
slipping languidly
through the window

Jeweled Sunrise

deep at the horizon
the sunrise is
a jewel in the ring
of the night...

When at the Ocean

when at the ocean
under the breaking waves
the whistling winds
the whooshing sand grains
one hears an undertone
like an ancient drum
the beat of the Universe –
a deep low hum…

Blue Irises

in the steaming mist
perked
blue irises
disrupting the waking mind's
penchant for order

III: TO MY LOVED ONES

"If you leave tomorrow
I will kiss you and tell you:
"Good luck…"
If you return thereafter
I will kiss you and tell you:
"Welcome back…"
Daniel, my Love, my Life

PASSION

I am the sand
You are the Ocean...
Coming

***

I am the cliff
You are the Ocean
Waves

DEAR BEAR

I know this is a special day –
For any day with you is special,
Just like the day when twenty-years-away
I met a boy with drive and passion.

Life then took us on a train
Through stations, oceans, flights and years
When our love alone remained
To take us through some lonely tears…

I know it's half a life away,
For half a life we've been together
And you have grown into a man
And I have grown even better…

Back then I looked into your eyes
And saw the future we are now having,
How was I going to deny –
I wanted to look in them forever.

And now, don't wish the time to stop
For I want more of this adventure,
Some other day ahead I hope,
We'll find how love had all the answers.

A STAR IS BORN

Every night above the roof
of the neighboring house
a star is born
out of the embrace
of the distant waves
pounding the horizon
with muted sounds
reaching the shore
calming the wild.

I'm wondering
Is it still in to stargaze?...
And yet every night transfixed
at my window sill
I watch the spectacle –
it outshines clouds
magnificent, upward
it goes in veils of nebular gauze
in its orbit night after night
so distant so close…

When I was a child
an LP revolving
with a nostalgic squeak
the Little Prince's
crystal
laughter:
"just look at the sky
if you miss me and I
will be there
and all the stars will be wells
and will give you fresh water to drink..."

A DAY OF LOVE

I lit up a cigarette
The smoke piling out the window
Along with the steaming roofs
The waves breaking
In the near shore
The sound so familiar
So old
And still as if
I'm hearing it for the first time
Anew

Saying good night
To a star I befriended
A barking dog
Going his own way
In the dusk...
It is a day
I want to remember
Because it is a day
Of love...

THE RAIN IS FALLING

The rain is falling
Silently in large drops
Splashing gently in the leaden puddles
Falling over meetings
And departures
Falling over our
Colored raincoats
Over trees
Exploding white and rose
Swimming in milky fog
Over an island
Which suddenly became so close...
Watering down memories and time.
And I am
Here and there
Somewhere in roaming
A distant shore
Silver lagoons at sunset
Light sipping through the haze at dusk
Over the bay
And lakes of melted silver
Reflect the final rays...

But the herons
Perched white amongst the reeds
Waiting for the dark to come along
And cover their wet
Asylums

KALEIDOSCOPE
to my dearest Tati & Vali

Sometimes we lose sight
Of the important things in our lives
We get used to it
They become trite
But if only you put your hands in front
                               of your forehead
And make a tiny window
Between your palms
And start turning around toward
Different objects in your surroundings
You suddenly have a kaleidoscope
To examine the things that
Come in your view
The objects
Start to shine
They become alive and new
And exude their innate light
Your books
Your child's drawings
Your wedding pictures
Your hometown photo
Your child's baby photo
Your child's end of year school photo
Your potted garden on the sun porch
A gift from your brother
A museum exhibit brochure
Left-over flowers your husband gave you
                               for your special day
Your cat stretching
Musical note sheets
A painted piece of wood
From your daughter
With an inconspicuous sign for only you to see,

Written in your mother's language
Which she's trying to learn
With a sweet spelling typo:
"Обичъм те!"...

CHEST COLD

My chest is cold
Without you loving me
Cold's sitting in my chest
'Cause you don't come at night to me
Cold is my chest
It misses your caress
My chest got a cold
Of love untold
Of feelings suppressed
Back down in my chest...

I AM YOUR TOWN

I am your town
But it was not built for you,
I am
Your flower
But in was not planted for you
I am here for you
As you're here for me
But don't pluck me out
Others also need me

MONDAY SONG

Don't go away from me
I will be sad
I will be sad without your hands
Don't go away from me
Today I will make
The most terrible
Delivery…

The rivers run dry
In their beds
The shores are
Deserted islands
When you're not here with me…

Don't go away from me
I will be gloomy
I will be blue without
Your eyes
Don't go away from me
Today I will deliver
The most terrible
Reverie…

There are no rivers
Under the bridges
The anchors hold no ships
When you're not here with me...

Don't go away from me
I will be sad
Without your hands...

DUET

She said, "I'd like to talk."

He said, "We talked already."

"What did we talk about?" – she asked.

He said, "You asked me, are you hungry?
I said, " I am."

You asked me, "What can I make you?
I asked, "What you have?.."

She smiled... laughed...

Her laughter falling like rose petals over his ears.

Then they talked about poetry,
                                      language and words...

THE POEMS I'VE GIVEN AWAY

The poems
I've given away
Are laying somewhere in
Drawers and files
Over two or perhaps more continents and isles
In two, three, or more
Different languages

Or perhaps they've become dust
And traveled miles
To conflate with the universal
Dust
Perhaps they are revolving
Around the Asteroid belt
Circling the sun
Perhaps they went
Into the ocean and fed
A crustacean
Perhaps they became
The base of the creation of
A new life, new idea
New thought
New cycle
Anything at all
That propelled something through

Or perhaps they were just recycled...
Perhaps, just perhaps they remained
In someone's heart
Forever tucked away
As fragile china
In the cupboards of the soul...

But I know the poems I've given
Away are not with me
I know

TEN BALLONS
to Vali on her birthday

Ten balloons –
Ten happy years celebrating you today!

Ten Balloons –
Ten sweet tears
Running down my happy face…

Ten pink roses –
Ten lovely smiles
Shining on your lovely face,
Ten pink roses,
Each one a blessing for you, child,
That I have you in my days...

Ten balloons –
Each one a year
Filled with joy and laughs and tears,
I'm holding their strings today
They're gently pulling
Up and away…

I will open my hand one day
To let you fly high and away…

But then and when we are apart
I will always have one big balloon
Filled with love and joy for you –
My heart!

TO MY MOM

For keepsake
From a land where
Ocean borders with the sky
And very often
Turned upside down
Pounds the roof
Of our house
For keepsake from a place
Where many evenings
We dreamed away
The waves, the Moon,
The sunrises and the summer haze
Where sea gulls and tiny
Little birds
Are resting on the rocks
And sands
And it's so quiet that sometimes
One hears the swishing of its grains
You hear your thoughts
Take off the surf
Beyond
The other side of the abyss

For keepsake from a piece of land
Standing on the whim of fate
Which sheltered us
And our children
And our hopes
And our curses
Accepted with open embrace

And because
This side of Earth
Will keep

Your fleeting bright
Moments with us
And ours with you
Forever...

HEART LEFT BEHIND

I have been gone for a while
Without ever leaving
I wandered the planes of the heart
With a heart left behind
It was lonely and desolate there
Barren...
I am back
Not a goddess for you
Not a priestess
I am here,
The woman with whom you remained
Who takes you beyond any pain
Beyond any memory

You'd know if
She loved you
when you find her
where you left her

Don't be gone for long –
The heart left alone
Will wander...

TELL THEM

"You cannot love me..."
"Tell this to the blossoming trees, opening under the warmth of the sun of first spring..."

"Stop wishing for me."
"Tell this to the running mountain stream, sliding over rocks, aiming for the sea..."

"Others might get hurt."
"Tell this to the wind that blows the earth, pushing boats from their moorings and causing floods..."

"We can never be together"
"Tell this to the ocean that caresses the shore, ever coming and going and coming back for more..."

They can never be one, yet cannot be apart,
forever aiming, forever departing
since the beginning of time...

IV. NEW ROMANTICS

Name your poems – don't leave them like orphans…

POETRY CORNER

Poetry comes to me
as the leaves come to a tree
relentless singing
my heart is wringing…
Give me a word, a phrase, a rhyme
I will transform it to abide
some ancient law
in arcane scribe...
In poetry and love and war,
There are no laws
Every poem that is read
anew interpreted
will resonated
like pristine bird song
when the sun is swimming out
from below its nightly loins
the poems falling from a tree
like leaves and taken by the breeze
will lay to earth
with wistful ease
What will be
Shall be
Shall be

LOVE IS...

when suddenly you recognize someone's perfume on your hands;
when you start saying things you don't mean;
when you feel happy or sad with everyone around...

When the clock measures the eternity until the next meeting...

Also when your brain is empty
empty empty
and it's only him

IS IT AN ANCIEN INCANTATION?

Tango embodies the nature of desire.
Striving, craving, coveting, longing, pining, abandoning....

Desire is about desiring,
not about achieving.
Desire is.

TANGO IS

Desire
Abandon
a spell
Spell
Thighs brushing
Wakening deep in
The well of the beginnings
Where desire.
Is. substance.
eternal aim
toward connection
of all things
atoms
and nuclei
in every cell
weak with exhaustion
strong
with drive

TO THE TANGO LESSON

Every time I walk the steps
And coming ever near
My heart's so beating in my chest
I feel you're going to hear
I fear when I step inside
My feet will melt like South
And by the time I tell you "Hi"
My voice will dry and halt.

But when you take me in embrace
Swirling me around
I feel at ease with every step
And taken with the sound,
The rhythm pulsing
Between us
Is thick with our vibration
And nothing else is in the world
But our rapt connection...

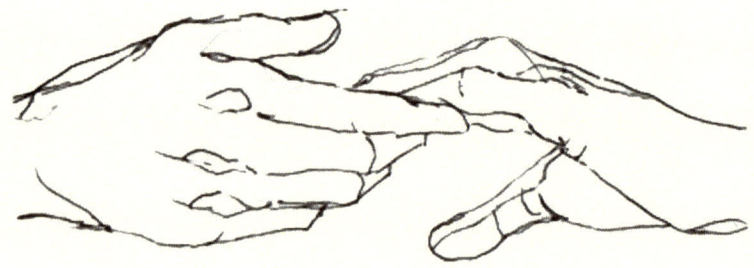

MORNING RHYTHM

I wish to get out
Without being hurt
Your art is the movement
My art is the word

They both have the rhythm
In common
And though
One is for body
The other for the mind
They're both for the soul…
They're both for the soul…

When I'm in your arms
And we're swaying in synch
That rhythm is rising
Deep from within
Swells up to my belly
My lungs and my heart
And stays with me long
After we've come apart...

And then I will carry
That rhythm so light
And it is transforming me
From the inside

My soul is now singing
In hope of reprieve
In hope that my spirit
Won't wander in grief...

You gave me your rhythm
I'm giving you mine
And let all the sorrows
Melt out in time...
Melt out in time.

I SEE SADNESS IN HIS EYES

I see sadness in his eyes
Swimming from bellow
Sometimes I sense
A wistful gaze
Gleaming ever slow
When suddenly I turn around
He shifts his gaze aside
I see something profound in him
That he's trying to hide…

Where have you been
Where have you gone
Where has your spirit wandered?

Have you a home
A kindred soul
To share in your candor…

Because my spirit
Let unbound
Is brooding far away
Come back to me
Come back to me
And let that moment stay

When through the eyes
And through the touch
And through your left my right
You suddenly unhinged a door
Led down to my insight
Led down to my very core
I did not know was barred

Now if I keep the door unbarred
You alone can come inside
From near and from far...

CORAZON

titillating
through my every neuron
how am I ever gonna
live without this
corazon a corazon
like a first kiss
like platonic longing
for a first beloved
who won't come back
I don't know how to let go
I don't know how to stay
pray for me
if you can pray
you are the one who's in control
and I'm the one who has to abandon all
that I knew
cannot let my heart go
just to watch it burn
just so it'd be a lesson learned...
but did I really learn

AFTER THE TAKEN

His crackling voice
is etching trails in my heart
trails traveled
but forgotten
sets my mind racing
I wish to reach out
on the wave of my thoughts
pacing back and forth
in my house
I lit up a cigarette
(have not smoked in a while)
I think of his image
I saw back then
on the empty street
on the distant isle
where somehow life had thrown me
it is
when I connected
with his world
and now
it is only the continuation
as if
some unknown roads
of innate intention
have crossed
interconnected
from continents
lost or rejected
in a new world...

PLEA

I have the time
You have the sparks
Tonight to make it count
For poetry and muses
Rhymes, for gazing at stars...
Instead I'm gazing solo

I tried, I really tried
To take you off my mind
I woke up every morning
With resolve I will be fine
But as the day drove to a close
Your image crystallized
Above my daily chores
My body weightless threw itself
On the wave of the thought of you
For love...

For love is reckless bold
And shameless
Bacchanalian of the night
Release me now
Before I fall and while still
I have some strength inside my mind,
release my heart...

LOVE IS ONLY FOR THE BRAVE

Love is only for the brave
Not for the faint of heart
Who is to say which love is right
And which one is not...

When love does find us
We may run away
Or we might try to hide
Is it a crime to dive in love
Or is it a crime to hide?..

Love is only for the strong
It is a mighty power
That sweeps us up
And throws us down
Within a single hour
Hopes and doubts, pining,
Pain, passion, bliss and sorrow,

All contained in love
And love cannot wait for tomorrow
To put on hold, to pass
As love is also fleeting
Can take us for a lifelong ride
Or die in single meeting...

PORTRAIT

He's sitting right across from me
in the afternoon sun
soft light streaming over his shoulders
he talks about the borders
he talks about the people's rights
he talks about the land he loves
and sparkles glimmer in his eyes
he really tries to get across
and make me realize his cause,
Surveying history and stories
He's earnest, he believes
in his stance,
he glows...
His lips are sculpting every word
his voice is swishing in my ears
I'm not sure what exactly I hear
but all I know is that he cares...
And all I want is to reach
my bare hands
across the border that's between us
and lay a kiss upon the scar
etched on his forehead
that looks like star...

NO HIDING IN THAT ONE

Mondays use to be mundane
Use to be so trite and grey
Even on a sunny day
Clouds gathering above
Clouds hanging in my groove
Even if there was no rain
Sometimes I wished
There was

Mondays aren't grey anymore
Even when there is a storm
Even when there is a flood
In my neighborhood

Because I get to see you then
Because you move me in your refrain
Because you talk to me with passion
No matter what – of Trump
Or fashion
Because you stir me
In so many ways
Mondays became my favorite days...

IN THE EMBRACE

His hair – raven wings
bracing his sides,
his eyes – dark-brown jaspers
smoldering below
his high aiming forehead,
his lips – slight upward curve
adorning a determined jaw
and then the straight line
of his shoulders
the gentle strength
at his arms
ending in graceful wrists
with soft palms and fine fingers,
gently holding mine...

NIGHT SONG

I wish the moon
Stays out longer
Does not get bleached
By morning light
Because the night
Because the night
The night
Of love
Is our night
When we will meet
Unknown to no one
Will float over the
Roofs and sea
And when the morning comes
No longer
Will we be able to see
What had transpired
I know
You're peering
At the
Moonlit face
Where our glances
Will collide
And when the dawn comes
No longer
Will we be able to abide
To stringent laws
I know
I know

SAY WHAT YOU WILL

I feel so settled and contained
I bought myself a bottle of
Champagne
put blackberries in it
and took the first sip.

The bubbles rolled down my throat
each one exploding in
a memory
of something I forgot

"Remember when ...
remember then ..."

I also remembered
I have a friend
who's probably sitting
in his chair
staring at the trees
swayed by the evening breeze
probably over a glass of wine
his thinking of what he's left behind
and what lays ahead
I'm glad I met him
as I know he's a caring person after all
and makes me happy and fulfilled
to have him
in my field
of dreams...

Say what you will
but I just feel
this bottle of champagne

is sipping in my brain
just fine...

POT OF MILK

I want to be your pot of milk
that on the stove is simmering –
every time you need a cup
you'll find it hot and steamy

That needs some tending,
I understand, to stay in that condition
one needs to watch attentively
and stir with repetition

Then you'll have a cup of cream
with tender top and flavorful steam
every sip will be delight
till the end of the night…

V. ODES

ODE ABOUT AN OLD CROW

Let me tell you about Alma Smith
Not any Alma Smith, but the one who lived up the street
She roused every morning and went for a ride
In her little red car that she rode in with pride,
With her snow-white hair always high in a bun
She sat in her wicker front chair
In the afternoon sun…

Oversized earrings adorned her face
Which exuded so much light and compassion and grace
For all that surrounded her
For the whole world
For the birds and the cats and the dogs and the squirrels
And the warmth and the cold and the wind
                                        and the snow –
Alma Smith had her door always open for them all…

She always adorned her house and front deck
For each and every holiday and season and event
With whimsical stuff, all so happy and bright
In the fall with the hay, on Christmas with the lights,
In spring with the blossoms and in summer with the flags,
For campaigns with the slogans, for Halloween with the rags…

When I passed by, I'd look to see if she's there
Because just a look at her place and white bun sticking over the chair
Brought such a joy no matter the day
For a life that is worth rising up to every day…

Sometimes in the evening I would see her inside
Looking quietly over the table
Under large stained-glass light
And I wondered what life, or photos, or spouse
She remembers alone in the dusk of her house…

One day I passed by and did not see her there –
The house was still decorated with flair
And I passed and I looked, but she was not inside.
Well, I thought, she must have gone for a ride…
Or maybe, she is gone for the day
Or just gone for a while someplace else to stay…

Some time passed, I found out she did go for a ride
Only this time it was to that…other side…

I did not know Alma Smith
But I can say
That I knew her in this inexplicable way
That she taught me a lesson not ever speaking a word
How to live and to love and experience this world
How to cherish every day, passer-by, every tree
And the bees and the flowers in the heat and the breeze
How there's reason to rise up every day with the sun
And to go back in the evening
And rise again with the dawn…

Feel the rhythm of seasons and the change and the awe
Of Nature and the offerings She has for us all…

And all that with a humor so astute and wry
For a little old lady of ninety-five
Who had a sign at her door throughout the year
That read:
"An Old Crow Lives Here" …

LITTLE BEIGE PANTS

Little beige pants
Plain blue shirt
Her hair demurely in a ponytail
She was picking her mail
And sending some off...
Running her daily routine
The kids and the shopping
Lunches and dinners,
Dry cleaners...
But all she could think of was love...

Her husband, he was a decent man,
They had been high school sweethearts
They took off to college
Wrote letters to each other
And promised to never be apart.

That's how it was,
After a while
Back to their hometown in Spring
They met and he said
He cannot live another
Day without her. And he offered a ring.

She said "yes!" so excited,
The young girl delighted in what it was there to come.
They married in Fall, rather fast
Went to honeymoon
Made love for the first time
Happy together at last.

Then the house, first child
In a year another
And a third
Life was busy and sweet,
Christmases rolled

One after another,
Thanksgivings and winters and springs...

At night, when the children were all put to bed
She stood in the kitchen to rest
Life has been good to her
Yet some deep vague regret
Was raising into her chest.

Of something un-lived
Something unknown
Something that has slipped away
She could not put her finger on it
And yet it was more distinct then her dinner plate.

Her body was young
She had vigor and strength
She could have traveled
The world
Could have had any man
Could have made love under the moon.

Love...
Was it that thing that they had
Back when they wed
Was it real,
Was it now gone?...
Was it all that there is to discover in this
Or perhaps there was something more,
Something profound
What the poets have sung
And maidens have run to
That she might have never found...

She would brush off the thought,
She'd drift into sleep
Taking check in her mind
Of the next day's daily chores.

Come morning again
She'd take up the day
Put her hair back in a ponytail,
Beige pants, blue shirt
She'd pass by the church
In her heart she'd silently pray
To release her from sin
She felt from within
For the love that her soul had craved...

THE DAY IS LONG

It starts so suddenly with the alarm clock
I put one foot down
Then another
Off to the kitchen
Turn the coffee pot on
The aroma will soon fill the room
Familiarly soothing and stimulating at once
The first sip is bliss
And then time for the breakfast feast
I like breakfast time
I like breakfast
Like the foods and goods that are offered
Especially eggs
But not until a cup of coffee
Is finished
But there is no feast
It's fast and efficient
I got to put some food
In my daughter's tummy
And in her lunch bag for lunch
I will not see her till the afternoon
And afternoon is way ahead
What's next?
Should I go back to bed...?
Sometimes my first thought when I get up is how
        I will do just that.
I never do
No, lied, I do sometimes if I had a very late night
        or early morning
Should I say,
"The day belongs to the night before" –
My husband says
He likes to stay late
Or early
Sometimes I'd get up and see him in the dim light
Hunched over his phone

Laughing at his favorite show
Why not come to me...?
He says "go, go to sleep"
And I do
He goes to bed and I get up,
He'll keep sleeping till the afternoon
And I'll keep quiet.
But back at the start...
At this point sun's shining high
Time to head down to the shore line
That moment when I reach the beach
                      can save the day for me
It's a shrine
I've created
That protects me from the day's chores
Hey, who can ask for more?
Living right here on the shore
It's been a blessing.
At first, I had no feelings towards
That sandy line
I was a mountain girl
But years passed by and I started craving
The dewy mornings in any season
So constant and so changing
At first, I always needed trees and forest
But now the sea's become my fortress
The jetty stones are my thrones
And seagulls almost seem like cousins
The waves are calming even in storms
The dunes, the reeds can be my shelter...
But where was I
Time to go back to the daily tasks
It's not even lunch time yet
I already had
Half of my day's emotions packed in this
                            early motion
Now what to prepare
Dishes, food, the fridge is sanctuary

With all the pictures from the years
And magnets from places far and near
Silly faces from events
Notes for school and notes for work
Calendar with wisdom phrases
Datelines that I need to meet.
Opening the fridge
Puts me on a ridge of memories
I drift away and then the rhymes start coming
Grab a pen or phone
Anything would work as long as I can put it down soon
Because after a while
It will melt away with the morning haze and evaporate
Then I'll search the words in vain
Lunch time – dishes, food, prepare
Time's running out I still stare at the pages
Fine I'm done
Let's get to it
Somehow lunch is mastered too
Phone calls managing appointments, check book,
                                                    bills are out
Well, maybe now I can have my breakfast…
Not sure what happens here
By the time the school bus comes near
And my girl's back with a storm
Not really
She's quiet more times than wild
She'll have her late lunch she calls dunch
After my husband is up
(He works late so don't mind that)
Coffee for him and a banana
I know his routine
It's nice to know
And not expect anything new

Some petty talk, the fridge, the bills,
                                          sometimes the news
    Sometimes a trill…

Wait, when was that?..
I almost forgot, yes, sure when our girl is sleeping over
We'll have a date,
But today's not that kind of day
Today's the familiar kind of day
Soon it will be time for work
And I am making him his lunch
Or rather dinner
His time is twisted
You see, he works late and we run in different plains
Sometime I'll go out of mine and he out of his
To meet me and then it's nice
We'll have this long and lively talks
All the world will melt around
We'll light a candle
Pour the liquor and on the flicker of the light
We'll talk till morning light and birds start singing
I don't like them birds singing so early
Before the sun had shown its face
They start to cheer
With clear voices
Which means it's time for us to stop
Put the blinds down and go
To sleep,
But I'll wake up in an hour
And he'll just snore till afternoon and I'll keep quiet
But where was I
The afternoon is running high
I have so much that's left behind
Unfinished I need to catch up
Some more chores
Thank goodness it is not a shopping day
Though sometimes I do like that
I'd rather be out in my car
Put the music on and while crossing the bridge
Pretend that I'm going somewhere away
Until I reach the produce store
We need potatoes, apples, more...

All right, that's done
He's gone for work
I'm settled –
Two of my missions are worth the day
To meet my daughter and send him away to work
                                        with his lunch
Then...it's my time...
I sit on the sun porch
My space with the orchids and flower pots
                                        and my work
In the branches of two big trees
I am in a tree house here
I can be anywhere in the world from here...
This might be the best part of the day
I can read and write and play
And I do...
Dusk moves slowly from the west,
From my windows I can see
Nuance of the setting sun
I can hear the evening breeze playing with the sea
Succumbing to the falling night
Now I can even sit outside
After all the island rains had rained themselves out
And wait for the stars to shine
For the moon to come out
On the one side of the house is the setting sun
On the other
The rising moon
And this is my price
For the day
That moment of change or turnover
Then it's when I can get beyond in that sliver,
A gap in the texture of time
Between day and night
When magical things can happen
I don't know what as I might find out the next day
I just try to write
And record those events

As they're fleeting
Soon will be time for bed
No, not for me
For my girl
She's in school the next day
She never wants to sleep
She's tiny
But it seems her mind is as active as mine
Takes some time to put her to sleep
Used to be with a song or a book we read
Now she wants to read or draw
I wait till there is no sound at her door
Then I still have some time left on my own
Back to my back window
The moon window
Where every cloudless night
The moon glares
And rises
Above the horizon
To move over the roof and beyond
And the stars and the fog
More often than not
This island is foggy or muggy and humid
I have grown to love this wetness
Enveloping drenching everything and in the morning
Slowly steaming from the earth and the ocean
But wait, it is not morning yet,
There is much left unsaid
Moon and stars are still out
Time to think and to dream
And to drink
To that
Until my eyelids
Start falling down
And I lay my head on the pillow
To wait for the alarm clock to ring...

VI. DREAMS

"The day belongs to the night before…"
Daniel

Dream I

Spacious open loft
Darkish Space With No Doors
Solid Dark Wood furniture
Modern with primitive mix
Luxuriously
Decadent
I'm thinking
Now I'm stuck here
How will I ever leave?
I will have to leave this to my child
She will be stuck here
I'm thinking:
How will I ever warm this place
Come winter...

Dream II

Two-leveled terminal
A shady Italian guy
Selling train tickets.
With some haggle
I get a ticket for the lower level
Where I need to go
The train rests in waiting
Long, Black
Its windows glistening
Like an ancient snake
Breathing
I alone mount it
It starts winding ahead
To an unknown destination
I feel settled and fulfilled...

A Dream in Film Noir

Walking the streets of a city alone,
mid evening, hazy and dark air
the mood is film noir
black & white
with hints of muted color
I swerve into an alley
in a deep corridor
with movie theater doors along the walls.
The titles of the movies are listed on the pilling
                                  brick walls,
young dapper intellectuals
are filling the corridor
against the walls.
I look to see which movie
I have not seen –
there are some with foreign titles,
looks like I've seen them all.
Continuing to the bottom of the corridor
                              I see the last door
and look inside the hall –
There are musicians there
seemingly preparing
for a rehearsal.
I feel the need to go in there
though I have no instrument
but only a hand bag
which I am very aware of carrying.
A person with Jewish kippah
looks out the door
to see if there are any more people to get in.
I hurriedly ask what movie is on.
He says, "Oh, these are short films,
5- minute ones
Tickets are fifty cents."
He ushers me in
not interested in the three dollars

I am trying to hand him.
I get in and walk with everyone
to another auditorium
in the back –
it is tight, but light
looks like a
university library
with desks.
As I walk through with a swing
under the gazes of man
I sit in the back row
slightly aroused
and wait for the picture to begin...

VII. TRANSLATED POEMS

*"With every gaze toward the Stars
The Earth becomes a little lighter"
My Father*

I Loved You
by Alexander Pushkin
(1829)

I loved you, my love is probably
still not entirely burned out in my soul.
But I don't want to cause you agony;
let it not bother you anymore.

I loved you silently, hopelessly,
at once the joy, the jealousy to thwart;
I loved you so honestly, so tenderly,
let God give way to others to your heart.

Prayer
by Mikhail Lermontov
(1829)

Don't hold against me, Lord Almighty,
Don't scold me, please, I beg of you,
That I'm in love with Earthly Darkness
With all her Passions and the Dirt...
That I don't often let the healing
Of your Word enter in my Soul,
That my thoughts are prowling freely
Away from You
In my misleading...

Don't hold against me, Lord Almighty,
That Passion's roaring on my chest,
That Inspiration strikes me wildly
And dims my eyes and senses...
My world is small for me, imperfect,
I fear You, but You are far,
I often seek my day's Salvation in sinful songs
                                  that are sub-par...

But take from me that mighty flaming,
That force that carries me along...
Keep me away from thirsty yearning
Turn my heart into a stone...

From constant longing for a singing,
Release me, Lord, once and for all,
And when I'm free from earthly sinning
I'll head towards Your Path once more...

Song of My Song
by Peyo Yavorov

At last you're coming back, oh harlot wretched,
with a bowed head –
to my dejected loneliness tonight.
Do not look back
where dark words echo
of fear and worry –
I know it all...
But you should also know:
the devil and the god back there died.

Come to me. Come in me.
And tell me:
Where were you not,
where was I not with you along?
Zigzags elusive everywhere...
When in my jealousy I burned
in summer heat,
and winter cold?

And with the ragged laborer, pale hungry,
in his shattered cellar were you not there –
and were you not lying to him, the poor,
for the holiday, for the sky and for the air?
And in the field,
with a rough peasant
were you not there next to him,
didn't you waste your days
and laugh at your own dreams?

And here, you're coming back scared,
exhausted, broken and despaired.
...The drunken lips of many
have sucked your ruby lips.
And dirty hands unraveled, tangled, spoiled
the silk of your hair.

In bloody embrace
how many times you bent?
Did I hear debauchery
your innocence submersed
your innocence poured down in
                      blasphemy and curse?

And here, you're coming back scared,
exhausted, broken and disappeared.
Do not look back –
there isn't anyone alive
in the crowds of the dead:
the only one remained
the fleshless ghosts, barely
visible in silence
in memory of fog.

A rascal, after you I went
and thought:
what does she love and hate?
Powerless in my jealousy, strong in my malice was I
and asked:
what lusts you, what attracts you?
Your voice silenced my steps wherever I go.
And I was searching
              I was searching then –
the instantly captured souls.

In vain I searched the truth within,
created in the lies and sin.
In vain I searched for the falsehood –
god of the universe, soul within soul.
Suffering! Only suffering remained
pitiful, indifferent,
there in the middle
of the truth and the falsehood ...

And here I am today:
you see – my loneliness a lonely peak.
And you came back, my beautiful!
Because there is no evil, suffering or life
beyond that heart of mine- a nod,
where the ashes reside
of all the truths and lies.
Because there is no soul or thing
beyond my chest - a furnace burning
with the living universal flame,
a temple of the universe contained.

And you came back! – Oh, holy day...
I will exhale a bloody flame,
I will burn here tree and rock.
Remain with me – be within me...
Amongst the bloody flame and smoke
amongst the suffocating haze,
wild sky's reflecting in your gaze.
My soul will crave the sky alone!
You gaze upwards,
sing me a song
of coolest rest, of emptiness.

Amongst the flames and hellish churn
with you together we will burn.
Beautiful in a dark embrace,
and ugly in a shining grace –
amongst unbearable suffocation,
longing for heavenly salvation,
with you along, we'll burn together,
my lonely song!

Two Beatiful Eyes
by Peyo Yavorov

Two beautiful eyes. The soul of a child
In two beautiful eyes – music and lights
Don't ask and don't show promise, they,
My soul is praying, child,
My soul is praying!

Passion and despair
Will throw tomorrow upon them
The dusky veil of sin and shame…
The dusky veil of sin and shame
Would not be thrown upon them
By passion and despair…
My soul is praying child,
My soul is praying…

Don't ask and don't show promise, they! –
Two beautiful eyes.
Music and lights,
In two beautiful eyes.
The soul of a child…

Two Souls
by Peyo Yavorov

I am not living: I am burning.
Inconsolable in my chest
two souls are in a fight:
the soul of an angel and a demon.
They're breathing flames,
and flames are drying me inside.

And double flames are bursting where I touch,
even in stones I hear double hearts...
Wherever I go I always see splitting apart
strange faces disappearing in the dust.

And after me in dust the wind will blow
covering my trails: who knows to where?
I am not living – I am burning! –
and my trail will be the dust
in dark infinitude somewhere.

To Lora
by Peyo Yavorov (1906)

My soul is moan. My soul is cry.
Because I am a bird that has been shot:
to death my soul is being wounded,
wounded by love...
My soul is moan. My soul is cry.
Tell me what it means to meet and to divide?
And here I tell you: there is hell and sorrow –
                and in the sorrow – there is love!

Mirages are near – the road is far.
surprised she's laughing with the joy
of ignorance and greedy youth,
of sultry flesh and spirit light...
Mirages are near – the road is far:
when she stands before me in brightness
she stands, but does not hear
the one who greaves and cries –
she – flesh and spirit light!...

Gaze Toward the Stars
by Iliya Stoykov, my father

On the crossroads of the FATE
I'm flying on the wings of thoughts
I want to find the end
From where our beginning starts
And the beginning where
LIFE tangles its knots.

Seemingly, it's all familiar:
You're born, you live, you die...
But sometimes accidental flashes:
Cool summer night,
Stars reaching down your astonished sight,
Their gleaming vibrancy shines on
The divine striving of the soul.

You lay quiet on the grass
Almost forgetting you're alive.
The wind carries through the silent night
The moonlit song of watchful birds.
In an instant daily cares chased aside
You fall asleep with a glimmer in your eyes.

You're waking up. Your legs are heavy
From pain that they don't walk the pavement.
Again you take the Road of Fate
With joy you're moving ever slightly,
All weight discarded...

With every gaze toward the Stars
The Earth becomes a little lighter...

APPENDIX

LIST OF DRAWINGS BY PENKO PLATIKANOV:

Cover image: *Eden* – charcoal and carbon pencil, etude

All other images are drawings in charcoal and carbon pencil on paper:

p. 2: *Dancer*
p. 14: *Midday*
p. 30: *Decision*
p. 48: *Song*
p. 66: *Doubt*
p. 82: *Morning*
p. 88: *Atlas*

The artist Penko Platikanov can be contacted at www.penkoart.com

LIST OF DRAWINGS BY VALENTINA ASENOV:

p. 52: *Reach*, digital drawing, 2018
p. 68: *Mama*, pen on paper, 2018

NOTES:

Kaleidoscope includes a Bulgarian phrase "Обичъм те" unintentionally misspelled by my daughter, who is bilingual. It would translate loosely as "I luv you."

A Star is Born includes in the last stanza rephrasing of the words of the Little Prince from the namesake novel of Antoine de Saint-Exupéry. The title of the poem, inadvertently coincides with the namesake movie "A STAR IS BORN"; this is not an allusion, as the poem was written before the movie's release.

Monday Song is a loose translation of a Bulgarian pop-song from the 1980's "Adaptation" sung by Vasil Naidenov.

Corazon includes a line *"cannot let my heart go just to watch it burn just so it is a lesson learned...but did I really learn"*, which is an allusion to a stanza from a song by Alice Merton "Jealousy" from her album "No roots" 2017. The original stanza is: *"I let my heart go, just to watch it burn So I told myself it's a lesson learned But did I really learn?"* The allusion is an inter-textual communication, as the song "Jealousy" was playing while the poem Corazon was being created.

Miniatures and Haiku from the Shore chapter includes a variety of different style poems, which do not follow the traditional Haiku rule of 5-7-5 syllable structure; rather the Haiku style is an influence to the miniature poems, while some of them loosely resemble a traditional Haiku structure.

NOTES ON TRANSLATED POEMS:

I Loved You is a lyrical miniature "Я вас любил," by A.S. Pushkin; first published in 1830 (in Russian)

Prayer, "Молитва," by Mikhail Lermontov, first published in 1829 (in Russian)

Song of my Song, ***To Lora***, and ***Two Beautiful Eyes*** – by Peyo Yavorov, first published in 1904-1906 (in Bulgarian). Recent editions:
Пейо К. Яворов, *Избрани Стихове* София, Пан, 1996
P.K.Yavorov, *Selected poems*, Sofia, Pan, 1996

Gaze toward the Stars, by Iliya Stoykov, first published (in Bulgarian) in:
Илия Стойков, *И повече светлина по пътя*, 2016, Абагар, Велико Търново
English translation:
Iliya Stoykov, *And More Light on the Way*, Abagar Publishing, Veliko Tărnovo, 2018

ABOUT THE AUTHOR

Detelina Stoykova-Asenov is an educator, writer and a psychoanalyst residing in New Jersey. Her writing career began as a student in St. Cyric and St. Methodius University of Veliko Tarnovo in Bulgaria where she studied Bulgarian Philology-Language and Literature. She had been a journalist and a TV and radio reporter. Her scholarly articles were published in specialized literature in her native Bulgaria, as well as in the US. Upon immigrating to the US, Detelina studied and graduated with an MA in Psychoanalysis from BGSP-NJ. Detelina is currently working as an educator and an independent mental health professional.

www.ingramcontent.com/pod-product-compliance
Lightning Source LLC
Chambersburg PA
CBHW060837170426
43192CB00019BA/2809